Modular Knitting
Made Easy™

Designs by Andra Knight-Bowman

HOUSE of
WHITE
BIRCHES

PUBLISHERS
SINCE 1947

2

Table of Contents

Mod Bag,
page 10

Ocean Breeze Hat & Scarf,
page 6

Modular Men's Crew,
page 19

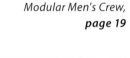

Perfect Summer Shell,
page 16

Winter Sky Hoodie,
page 31

Smart & Sassy
Dog Sweater,
page 42

Introduction

Oh, the fine art of modular knitting! How intriguing it is, but do not let it intimidate you. It's really quite simple.

Many people have asked me "Who invented this method?" In the 1940s, Virginia Wood Bellamy invented a new style of knitting, "number knitting," which she then had patented in 1948. This is commonly known today as modular knitting. She published a book on her patented knitting style in 1952. At that time, only square, rectangular or triangular pieces were made for throws or shawls. Over the years we have used and modified Ms. Bellamy's invention to make wearable garments!

I hope my creations bring great joy to all readers of this book, as I have had great joy in creating them.

Andra Knight-Bowman

Meet The Designer

At the age of 7, I learned to knit, and I was a natural at the craft. I soon started making sweaters for my Barbie dolls and my dog, Mitzi. Designing entered my life at an early age.

In high school, I had the opportunity to work at a local yarn shop; it was there I learned about fibers and sweater designing. My goal in life was to own a yarn shop of my own.

I opened Knits & Pearls in 2004 and introduced many of my designs from previous years to my customers. Since then I have created many more designs. They have been published in numerous magazines and a book titled *Easy Cable Knits for all Seasons*. I feel so blessed and am grateful for everyone who has believed in me.

I reside in Johnson City, Tenn., with my wonderful husband, Terry, who has been a gem through book writings and two furry kids (cats), Billie and Blue. I just couldn't ask for a better life!

Modular Knitting Step-by-Step

Thumb Method Cast-On

With yarn, make a slip knot on needle. Wrap yarn around thumb.

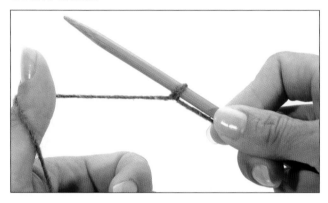

Slide needle through loop on thumb.

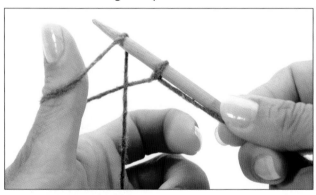

Repeat until 41 sts are on needle.

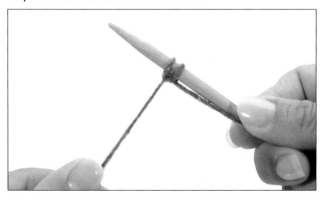

Block Pattern

Row 1 and all odd numbered rows (RS): Knit.

Row 2 (WS): K19, k3tog (see Photo A), k19.

Photo A

Row 4: K18, k3tog, k18.

Row 6: K17, k3tog, k17.

Row 8: K16, k3tog, k16.

Row 10: K15, k3tog, k15.

Row 12: K14, k3tog, k14.

Row 14: K13, k3tog, k13.

Row 16: K12, k3tog, k12.

Row 18: K11, k3tog, k11.

Row 20: K10, k3tog, k10.

Row 22: K9, k3tog, k9.

Row 24: K8, k3tog, k8.

Row 26: K7, k3tog, k7.

Row 28: K6, k3tog, k6.

Row 30: K5, k3tog, k5.

Row 32: K4, k3tog, k4.

Row 34: K3, k3tog, k3.

Row 36: K2, k3tog, k2.

Row 38: K1, k3tog, k1.

Row 40: K3tog—1 st remains on needle. Do not finish off.

Next Block

Row 1 (RS): Hold previous block with RS facing and rem st on needle, working along side of block in ends of rows, insert needle in end of row (Photo B), wrap yarn around needle, pulling up loop (Photo C). Continue to pick up sts in this manner to end of block for a total of 19 sts on the needle, cast on 21 sts using thumb method (Photo D).

Photo B

Photo C

Photo D

Rep Rows 2–40 of block pat.

Right Side

Wrong Side

Ocean Breeze Scarf & Hat

Designs by Andra Knight-Bowman

Skill Level

 EASY

Finished Measurements

Approx 5 x 45 inches, excluding fringe

Materials

- Plymouth Boku 95% wool/5% silk worsted weight yarn (99 yds/50g per ball): 2 balls variegated #10 (MC)
- Berroco Suede 100% nylon worsted weight yarn (120 yds/50g per ball): 1 ball Wild Bill Hickcock #3717 (CC)
- Size 9 (5.25mm) needles or size needed to obtain gauge
- Size H/8 (5mm) crochet hook (for attaching fringe)

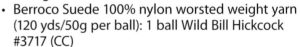

Gauge

16 sts and 32 rows = 4 inches/10 cm in garter st. To save time, take time to check gauge.

Pattern Notes

Use thumb method cast-on as shown on page 4 for entire project.

Scarf

Cast on 41 sts.

First Block

Row 1 and all odd-numbered rows (RS): Knit.

Row 2: K19, k3tog, k19.

Row 4: K18, k3tog, k18.

Row 6: K17, k3tog, k17.

Row 8: K16, k3tog, k16.

Row 10: K15, k3tog, k15.

Row 12: K14, k3tog, k14.

Row 14: K13, k3tog, k13.

Row 16: K12, k3tog, k12.

Row 18: K11, k3tog, k11.

Row 20: K10, k3tog, k10.

Row 22: K9, k3tog, k9.

Row 24: K8, k3tog, k8.

Row 26: K7, k3tog, k7.

Row 28: K6, k3tog, k6.

Row 30: K5, k3tog, k5.

Row 32: K4, k3tog, k4.

Row 34: K3, k3tog, k3.

Row 36: K2, k3tog, k2.

Row 38: K1, k3tog, k1.

Row 40: K3tog—1 st remains on needle. Do not finish off.

Second Block
Row 1 (RS): With RS facing, pick up and knit 19 sts in ends of rows along side of previous block, cast on 21 sts—41 sts (including st on needle from previous block).

Rows 2–40: Rep Rows 2–40 of First Block.

Third–Ninth Block
Work same as for Second Block.

At end of ninth block, fasten off.

Fringe
Cut 8-inch lengths of CC for fringe.

Work 7 knots across each end as follows: Hold 3 lengths of CC tog and fold in half. With RS of scarf facing, with crochet hook, draw folded end through edge stitch from right to wrong side. Pull loose ends through folded section and draw knot up firmly.

Hat

Skill Level
 INTERMEDIATE

Finished Size
Hat circumference: 21 inches

Materials
- Plymouth Boku 95% wool/5% silk worsted weight yarn (99 yds/50g per ball): 2 balls variegated #10 (MC)
- Berroco Suede 100% nylon worsted weight yarn (120 yds/50g per ball): 1 ball Wild Bill Hickcock #3717 (CC)
- Size 5 (3.75mm) 16-inch circular needle
- Size 9 (5.25mm) straight needles or size needed to obtain gauge
- Stitch marker
- Tapestry needle

Gauge
16 sts and 32 rows = 4 inches/10 cm with larger needles in garter st.
To save time, take time to check gauge.

Pattern Notes
Use thumb method cast-on as shown on page 4 for entire project.

Hat is worked in strips of gradually decreasing size blocks from band to crown.

It is helpful to place a small pin or marker on the right side of the first block.

Hat

Band
With smaller needles and CC, cast on 80 sts, place marker for beg of rnd. Join being careful not to twist sts.

Rnd 1: Purl.

Rnd 2: Knit.

Rnds 3–12: Rep [Rnds 1 and 2] 5 times. Leave stitches on needle.

First Strip

First Block
With larger needles and MC, knit next 10 band sts, cast on 11 sts—21 sts.

Row 1 (WS): K9, k3tog, k9.

Row 2 and all even-numbered rows (RS): Knit.

Row 3: K8, k3tog, k8.

Row 5: K7, k3tog, k7.

Row 7: K6, k3tog, k6.

Row 9: K5, k3tog, k5.

Row 11: K4, k3tog, k4.

Row 13: K3, k3tog, k3.

Row 15: K2, k3tog, k2.

Row 17: K1, k3tog, k1.

Row 19: K3tog—1 st remains on needle. Do not finish off. Turn.

Second Block

With RS facing, pick up and knit 7 sts in ends of rows along side of First Block, cast on 9—17 sts (includes st on needle at end of previous block).

Row 1 (WS): K7, k3tog, k7.

Row 2 and all even-numbered rows (RS): Knit.

Row 3: K6, k3tog, k6.

Row 5: K5, k3tog, k5.

Row 7: K4, k3tog, k4.

Row 9: K3, k3tog, k3.

Row 11: K2, k3tog, k2.

Row 13: K1, k3tog, k1.

Row 15: K3tog—1 st remains on needle. Do not finish off. Turn.

Third Block

With RS facing, pick up and 5 sts in ends of rows along side of Second Block, cast on 7 sts—13 sts (includes st on needle at end of previous block).

Row 1 (WS): K5, k3tog, k5.

Rows 2 and all even-numbered rows (RS): Knit.

Row 3: K4, k3tog, k4.

Row 5: K3, k3tog, k3.

Row 7: K2, k3tog, k2.

Row 9: K1, k3tog, k1.

Row 11: K3tog—1 st remains on needle. Do not finish off. Turn.

Fourth Block

With RS facing, pick up and knit 3 sts in ends of rows along side of Third Block, cast on 5—9 sts (includes st on needle at end of previous block).

Row 1 (WS): K3, k3tog, k3.

Row 2 and all even-numbered rows (RS): Knit.

Row 3: K2, k3tog, k2.

Row5: K1, k3tog, k1.

Row 7: K3tog—1 st remains on needle. Do not finish off. Turn.

Fifth Block

With RS facing, pick up and knit 1 st in end of row along edge of Fourth Block, cast on 3 sts—5 sts (includes st on needle at end of previous block).

Row 1 (WS): K1, k3tog, k1.

Row 2 (RS): Knit.

Row 3: K3tog.

Row 4: Knit.

Fasten off.

Second Strip

This strip is worked in ends of rows along the right edge of the previous strip. Slide next 10 sts to right of previous strip to larger needle, attach MC and knit these 10 sts, pick up and knit 11 sts in ends of rows of First Block of previous strip—21 sts.

Work Second through Fifth Block as for First Strip.

Third through Eighth Strip

Work same as for Second Strip. At end of Fifth Block on Eighth Strip, do not fasten off.

Crown

With RS facing, pick up and knit 15 sts across ends of rows of Fifth blocks—16 sts (includes st on needle at end of previous block).

Row 1 (WS): Knit.

Row 2 (RS): [K2tog] 8 times—8 sts.

Row 3: Knit.

Row 4: [K2tog] 4 times—4 sts.

Cut yarn leaving 6-inch tail. With tapestry needle, weave thread through rem sts and pull tightly.

Sew seam and weave in ends. ❖

Mod Bag

Design by Andra Knight-Bowman

Skill Level

■■■□ INTERMEDIATE

Finished Size
Approx 8½ high x 11 wide x 3½ deep

Materials
• Plymouth Galway Worsted 100% wool worsted weight yarn (210 yds/100g per ball): 3 balls green #145
• Size 7 (4.5mm) straight and double-point needles or size needed to obtain gauge
• Cable needle
• Tapestry needle
• 3½ x 11 inch piece of adhesive foam board for bottom (if desired)

Gauge
20 sts and 40 rows = 4 inches/10 cm in garter st. To save time, take time to check gauge.

Special Abbreviations
Cable Front (CF): Slip next 4 sts onto cable needle and hold in front of work, k4, k4 from cable needle.

Cable Back (CB): Slip next 4 sts onto cable needle and hold in back of work, k4, k4 from cable needle.

Pattern Notes
Use thumb method cast-on as shown on page 4 for entire project.

Bag is made by working cable panel for top edge first, then picking up stitches along the side of the cable for the modular blocks. Three blocks for the bottom are added to the second row of blocks and sewn to the remaining blocks.

Pattern Stitch
Cable Panel Pattern (multiple of 18 sts)

Row 1 (RS): K1, p2, k12, p2, k1.

Row 2 and all even-numbered rows: P1, k2, p12, k2, p1.

Row 3: K1, p2, CF, k4, p2, k1.

Row 5: Rep Row 1.

Row 7: K1, p2, k4, CB, p2, k1.

Row 8: Rep Row 2.

Rep Rows 1–8 for pat.

Bag

Cable Panel
Cast on 18 sts.

Work [Rows 1–8 of Cable Panel] 24 times. Bind off loosely.

Body

Row 1

First Block
Cast on 17 sts, holding cable panel with RS facing and working in ends of rows along edge of panel, pick up and knit 18 sts, picking up 3 sts for every 4 rows—35 sts. Turn.

Row 1 (WS): K16, k3tog, k16.

Row 2 and all even-numbered rows: Knit.

Row 3: K15, k3tog, k15.

Row 5: K14, k3tog, k14.

Row 7: K13, k3tog, k13.

Continue in this manner having 1 less st each side of the dec until 3 sts rem.

Next row: K3tog—1 st remains on needle. Do not finish off.

Second Block
With RS facing, pick up and knit 16 sts in ends of rows of previous block, pick up 18 sts along Cable Panel as before—35 sts (includes st on needle at end of previous block).

Work same as for First Block.

Third through Eighth Blocks
Work same for Second Block.

Row 2

First Block
Cast on 17 sts, with RS facing, pick up and knit 18 sts in ends of rows of First Block on previous row—35 sts. Turn.

Second Block
With RS facing, pick up and knit 16 sts in ends of rows along edge of previous block, pick up and knit 18 sts in ends of rows along edge of corresponding block on previous row—35 sts (includes st on needle at end of previous block).

Work same as for First Block.

Work rem blocks in Row 2 as for Second Block.

Fasten off.

Purse Bottom
Note: First, second and third blocks form one side of purse, fourth blocks forms one end; fifth, sixth and seventh blocks form opposite side and eighth block forms opposite end.

Work 3 blocks as for the first, second and third blocks of Row 2.

Assembly
Sew bottom to edges of rem blocks. Sew beg and ends of block rows and cable panel tog.

Strap
Work Rows 1–8 of Cable Panel pat for 30 inches.

I-cord bow
With double-point needles, cast on 5 sts.

Knit 1 row.

*Slide sts to the other end of needle, pulling yarn across back of work, knit; rep from * until I-cord measures 20 inches. Bind off.

Finishing
Sew purse handle ends at each side. Tie I-cord in a bow and tack on front of bag.

Place foam board in bottom of bag, if desired. ❖

Raspberry Diamonds Shawl

Design by Andra Knight-Bowman

Skill Level

 INTERMEDIATE

Finished Size

Diagonal edge: Approx 38 inches
Long edge: Approx 60 inches

Materials

- Berroco Bonsai 97% bamboo/3% wool worsted weight yarn (77 yds/50g per hank): 8 hanks Bito #4150
- Size 8 (5mm) straight and 32-inch circular needles or size needed to obtain gauge

Gauge

16 sts and 24 rows = 4 inches/10 cm in St st.
To save time, take time to check gauge.

Special Abbreviation

Central Double Decrease (CDD): Slip next 2 sts as if to k2tog, k1, pass 2 slipped sts over.

Pattern Notes

Use thumb method cast on as shown on page 4 for entire project.

Follow chart using the numbers as sequence for placement of blocks and letters as reference to the method used for working each block.

Slip stitches knitwise when knitting and purlwise when purling.

Shawl

Row 1

Block 1 (Method A)

With straight needles cast on 31 sts.

Row 1 and all odd-numbered rows (WS): Sl 1p, purl across.

Row 2 (RS): Sl 1k, ssk, yo, k11, CDD, k11, yo, k2tog, k1.

Row 4: Sl 1k, ssk, yo, k10, CDD, k10, yo, k2tog, k1.

Row 6: Sl 1k, ssk, yo, k9, CDD, k9, yo, k2tog, k1.

Row 8: Sl 1k, ssk, yo, k8, CDD, k8, yo, k2tog, k1.

Row 10: Sl 1k, ssk, yo, k7, CDD, k7, yo, k2tog, k1.

Row 12: Sl 1k, ssk, yo, k6, CDD, k6, yo, k2tog, k1.

Row 14: Sl 1k, ssk, yo, k5, CDD, k5, yo, k2tog, k1.

Row 16: Sl 1k, ssk, yo, k4, CDD, k4, yo, k2tog, k1.

Row 18: Sl 1k, ssk, yo, k3, CDD, k3, yo, k2tog, k1.

Row 20: Sl 1k, ssk, yo, k2, CDD, k2, yo, k2tog, k1.

Row 22: Sl 1k, ssk, yo, k1, CDD, k1, yo, k2tog, k1.

Row 24: Sl 1k, ssk, yo, CDD, yo, k2tog, k1.

Row 26: Sl 1k, k1, CDD, k2.

Row 28: Sl 1k, CDD, k1.

Row 30: CDD—1 st remains on needle. Do not fasten off.

Block 2 (Method B)

With RS of previous block facing and referring to chart for placement, pick up and knit 14 sts in ends of rows along edge of previous block, cast on 16 sts—31 sts (includes st left on needle at end of previous block).

Work same as Rows 1–30 of Block 1.

Blocks 3–8

Referring to chart for placement, work same as for Block 2 (Method B).

Block 9 (Method C)

With RS of previous block facing, pick up and knit 14 sts in ends of rows along edge of previous block, cast on 16 sts—31 sts (includes st left on needle at end previous block).

Row 1 (WS): Sl 1p, purl across.

Row 2 (RS): Sl 1k, ssk, yo, k11, CDD, k11, k2tog, k1.

Rows 3, 5, 7, 9, 11: Sl 1p, p2tog, purl to last 5 sts, p2tog, p1.

Row 4: Sl 1k, ssk, k9, CDD, k9, k2tog, k1.

Row 6: Sl 1k, ssk, k7, CDD, k7, k2tog, k1.

Row 8: Sl 1k, ssk, k5, CDD, k5, k2tog, k1.

Row 10: Sl 1k, ssk, k3, CDD, k3, k2tog, k1.

Row 12: Sl 1k, ssk, k1, CDD, k1, k2tog, k1.

Row 13: Sl 1p, p2tog, p3, p2tog, p1.

Row 14: Sl 1k, k1, CDD, k2.

Row 15: Sl 1p, p3tog, p1.

Row 16: CDD. Fasten off.

Row 2

Block 10 (Method D)

With RS of Row 1 facing and referring to chart for placement, cast on 16 sts, pick up and knit 15 sts in ends of rows along edge of corresponding block on previous row—31 sts.

Work same as Rows 1–30 of Block 1.

Block 11 (Method E)

With RS facing and referring to chart for placement, pick up and knit 14 sts in ends of rows along edge of previous block, pick up and knit 16 sts in ends of rows along edge of corresponding block on previous row—31 sts (includes st left on needle at end of previous block)

Work same as Rows 1–30 of Block 1.

Blocks 12–16

Work same as for Block 11.

Block 17 (Method F)

With RS facing and referring to chart for placement, pick up and knit 14 sts in ends of rows along edge of previous block, pick up and knit 16 sts in ends of rows along edge of corresponding block on previous row—31 sts (includes st left on needle at end previous block).

Row 1 (WS): Sl 1p, purl across.

Row 2 (RS): Sl 1k, ssk, yo, k11, CDD, k11, k2tog, k1.

Rows 3, 5, 7, 9, 11: Sl 1p, p2tog, purl to last 5 sts, p2tog, p1.

Row 4: Sl 1k, ssk, k9, CDD, k9, k2tog, k1.

Row 6: Sl 1k, ssk, k7, CDD, k7, k2tog, k1.

Row 8: Sl 1k, ssk, k5, CDD, k5, k2tog, k1.

Row 10: Sl 1k, ssk, k3, CDD, k3, k2tog, k1.

Row 12: Sl 1k, ssk, k1, CDD, k1, k2tog, k1.

Row 13: Sl 1p, p2tog, p3, p2tog, p1.

Row 14: Sl 1k, k1, CDD, k2.

Row 15: Sl 1p, p3tog, p1.

Row 16: CDD. Fasten off.

Rows 3–8

Blocks 18 – 44

Referring to chart for placement, work first block of each row as for Block 10 (Method D), rem whole blocks in row as for Block 11 (Method E) and end block as for Block 17 (Method F).

Row 9

Block 45 (Method G)

With RS facing and referring to chart for placement, cast on 16 sts, pick up and knit 15 sts in ends of rows along edge of first block of previous row—31 sts.

Work same as Rows 1–16 of Block 17.

Border

Hold shawl with RS facing and long edge at bottom. With circular needle and beg along diagonal side of the triangle, pick up 1 st in each st along 2 diagonal edges of shawl. Do not pick up sts along the long edge. Turn.

Row 1 (WS): Knit.

Row 2 (RS): K1, *yo, k2tog; rep from * across.

Row 3: Purl.

Bind off loosely knitwise. ❖

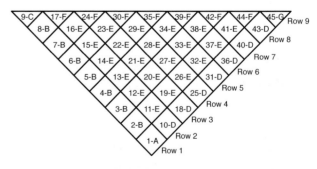

SHAWL CHART

Perfect Summer Shell

Design by Andra Knight-Bowman

Skill level

■■■□ INTERMEDIATE

Sizes

Woman's small (medium, large, extra-large, 2X-large) Instructions are given for smallest size, with larger sizes in parentheses. When only 1 number is given, it applies to all sizes.

Finished Measurements

Chest: 36 (40, 44, 48, 52) inches
Length: 22 (23, 24, 25, 26) inches

Materials

- Plymouth Jeannee Worsted 51% cotton/49% acrylic worsted weight yarn (110 yds/50g per ball): 9 (10, 11, 12, 13) balls yellow #17
- Size 6 (4.25mm) 16- and 32-inch circular needles
- Size 7 (4.5mm) needles or size needed to obtain gauge
- Cable needle
- Stitch holders
- Lock ring markers
- Tapestry needle

4 MEDIUM

Gauge

20 sts and 25 rows = 4 inches/10 cm with larger needles in St st.
To save time, take time to check gauge.

Special Abbreviations

Cable front (CF): Slip next 4 sts on cable needle, hold in front, k4, k4 from cable needle.

Cable back (CB): Slip next 4 sts on cable needle, hold in back, k4, k4 from cable needle.

Pattern Stitch

Cable Panel (worked over 18 sts)

Row 1 (RS): K1, p2, k12, p2, k1.

Row 2: P1, k2, p12, k2, p1.

Row 3: K1, p2, CF, k4, p2, k1.

Row 4: Rep Row 2.

Rows 5 and 6: Rep Rows 1 and 2.

Row 7: K1, p2, k4, CB, p2, k1.

Row 8: P1, k2, p12, k2, p1.

Rep Rows 1–8 for pat.

Pattern Notes

Use thumb method cast-on as shown on page 4 for entire project.

The cable for back/front is worked first. The body is worked with horizontal rows of blocks from one side of the Cable Panel to the lower edge (refer to Block Diagram for placement). The yoke is worked by picking up stitches along the opposite side of Cable Panel and working to the shoulder.

Back

Cable Panel

With larger needles, cast on 18 sts.

Work Rows 1–8 of Cable Panel pat for 120 (132, 146, 160, 172) rows.

Bind off loosely.

Body

Row 1

First Block

With larger needles, cast on 23 (26, 28, 31, 33) sts, with RS of Cable Panel facing, pick up and knit 22 (25, 27, 30, 32) sts along one edge Cable Panel picking up 3 sts for every 4 rows—45 (51, 55, 61, 65) sts. Turn.

Row 1 (WS): K21 (24, 26, 29, 31), k3tog, k21 (24, 26, 29, 31).

Rows 2 and all even-numbered rows (RS): Knit.

Row 3: K20 (23, 25, 28, 30), k3tog, k20 (23, 25, 28, 30).

Continue in this manner having one less st on each side of dec until 3 sts rem.

Next row: K3tog—1 st remains on needle. Do not finish off.

Second Block

With RS facing, pick up and knit 22 (25, 27, 30, 32) sts in ends of rows along side of previous block, then pick up 22 (25, 27, 30, 32) sts along Cable Panel pat as before—45 (51, 55, 61, 65) sts (includes st on needle from previous block). Turn.

Work same as for First Block.

Third and Fourth Block

Work same as for Second Block. At end of Fourth Block, finish off.

Rows 2 and 3

Work same as for Row 1 picking up sts in ends of rows of corresponding block in previous row instead of in Cable Panel.

There should be 12 blocks.

Yoke

With larger needles, RS facing and working along opposite side of Cable Panel, pick up and knit 90 (100, 110, 120, 130) sts, picking up at a rate of 3 sts for every 4 rows.

Knit 3 rows.

Work in St st until total length of piece measures 22 (23, 24, 25, 26) inches.

Place first 30 (34, 37, 40, 43) sts on a holder, place center 30 (32, 36, 40, 44) sts on a holder, place rem 30 (34, 37, 40, 43) sts on a holder.

Front

Work as for back until total length of piece measures 19 (20, 21, 22, 23) inches, ending with WS row completed.

Shape neck

Work across 35 (39, 42, 45, 48) sts, place center 20 (22, 26, 30, 34) sts on a holder, attach 2nd skein of yarn and work rem 35 (39, 42, 45, 48) sts.

Working both sides at once, continue in St st dec 1 st at each neck edge [every row] 5 times—30 (34, 37, 40 43) sts on each side.

House of White Birches, Berne, Indiana 46711

Continue even until piece measures same as back.

Assembly

Join shoulders with 3-Needle Bind-Off as follows: Place back and front with RS tog. Slide shoulder sts from the front onto a needle, slide shoulders sts from back onto another needle. Position front and back with needles facing in the same direction, with a third needle, knit a st from each needle tog, bind off at the same time.

Mark 7½ (8, 8½, 9, 9) inches down from shoulder on each side.

Sew side seams from markers to lower edge.

Neckband

With RS facing and 16 inch circular needle, beg at one shoulder seam, pick up and knit 82 (86, 94, 102, 110) sts around neck edge. Join, placing marker at beg of rnd.

Rnd 1: Purl.

Rnd 2: Knit.

Rnd 3: Purl.

Bind off loosely.

Armbands

With RS facing and 16-inch circular needle, beg at underarm seam, pick up and knit 78 (82, 86, 90, 90) sts around armhole opening.

Rnd 1: Purl.

Rnd 2: Knit.

Rnd 3: Purl.

Bind off loosely.

Bottom Band

With RS facing and 32-inch circular needle, beg at side seam, pick up and knit 132 (150, 162, 180, 192) sts around lower edge.

Rnd 1: Purl.

Rnd 2: Knit.

Rnd 3: Purl.

Bind off loosely. ❖

Cable Panel			
First Block	Second Block	Third Block	Fourth Block
Fifth Block	Sixth Block	Seventh Block	Eighth Block
Ninth Block	Tenth Block	Eleventh Block	Twelfth Block

Row 1, Row 2, Row 3

Block Diagram

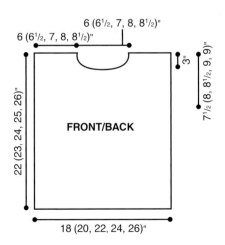

Modular Men's Crew

Design by Andra Knight-Bowman

Skill Level

■■■□ INTERMEDIATE

Sizes

Man's small (medium, large, extra-large, 2X-large) Instructions are given for smallest size, with larger sizes in parentheses. When only 1 number is given, it applies to all sizes.

Finished Measurements

Chest: 40 (44, 48, 52, 56) inches
Length: 27 (28, 29, 30, 31) inches

Materials

- Berroco Comfort 50% super fine nylon/50% super fine acrylic worsted weight yarn (210 yds/100g per ball): 8 (9, 10, 11, 12) balls smokestack #9729
- Size 6 (4.25mm) straight and 16-inch circular needles
- Size 8 (5mm) straight needles or size needed to obtain gauge
- Cable needle
- Stitch holders
- Lock ring markers
- Tapestry needle

Gauge

18 sts and 25 rows = 4 inches/10 cm in St st.
To save time, take time to check gauge.

Special Abbreviations

Cable front (CF): Slip next 4 sts on cable needle, hold in front, k4, k4 from cable needle.

Cable back (CB): Slip next 4 sts on cable needle, hold in back, k4, k4 from cable needle.

Pattern Stitch

Cable Panel (worked over 18 sts)

Row 1 (RS): K1, p2, k12, p2, k1.

Row 2: P1, k2, p12, k2, p1.

Row 3: K1, p2, CF, k4, p2, k1.

Row 4: Rep Row 2.

Rows 5 and 6: Rep Rows 1 and 2.

Row 7: K1, p2, k4, CB, p2, k1.

Row 8: P1, k2, p12, k2, p1.

Rep Rows 1–8 for pat.

Pattern Notes

Use thumb method cast-on as shown on page 4 for entire project.

Sweater back body is worked from side-to-side with vertical rows of blocks (see back block diagram). Yoke is worked by picking up stitches across the blocks and working toward shoulders.

Sweater front is made by working center cable panel first, then picking up stitches along each side of the panel for the modular blocks (see front block diagram). Yoke is worked by picking up stitches across blocks and working toward shoulders.

Back

With larger needles cast on 45 (49, 53, 57, 61) sts.

Row 1

Note: Rows of blocks are worked vertically from lower edge to yoke (see Block Diagram on page 23). Mark RS of First Block.

First Block

Row 1 and all odd-numbered rows (RS): Knit.

Row 2: K21 (23, 25, 27, 29) sts, k3tog, k21, (23, 25, 27, 29) sts.

Row 4: K20 (22, 24, 26, 28) sts, k3tog, k20 (22, 24, 26, 28) sts.

Continue in this manner having 1 less stitch on each side of dec until 3 sts rem.

Next row: K3tog—1 st remains on needle. Do not finish off.

Second Block

Row 1 (RS): With RS of facing, pick up and knit 22 (24, 26, 28, 30) sts in ends of rows along edge of previous block, cast on 22 (24, 26, 28, 30) sts—45 (49, 53, 57, 61) sts (includes st left on needle from previous block).

Beg with Row 2, work same as for First Block.

Third Block

Work same as for Second Block. At end of last row, fasten off.

Row 2

Fourth Block

Row 1 (RS): Cast on 23 (25, 27, 29, 31) sts, pick up and knit 22 (24, 26, 28, 30) sts in ends of row along side of corresponding block on previous row.

Beg with Row 2, work same as for First Block.

Fifth Block

Row 1 (RS): Pick up and knit 22 (24, 26, 28, 30) sts in ends of rows of previous block, pick up and knit 22 (24, 26, 28, 30) sts in ends of rows of corresponding block on previous row—45 (49, 53, 57, 61) sts (includes st left on needle from previous block).

Beg with Row 2, work same as for First Block.

Sixth Block

Work same as Fifth Block.

Rows 3 and 4

Work same as for Row 2—4 rows with 3 blocks in each row.

Yoke

Hold blocks with RS facing and side with 4 blocks at top. With larger needles, pick up and knit 85 (95, 103, 113, 121) sts across blocks at a rate of 3 sts for every 4 rows.

Knit 3 rows.

Change to St st and work until piece measures 24 (25, 26, 27, 28) inches ending with a WS row. Place first 30 (33, 36, 39, 42) sts on a holder, place center 25 (29, 31, 35, 37) sts on a holder, place rem 30 (33, 36, 39, 42) sts on a holder.

Waist ribbing

Hold blocks with RS facing and opposite side of blocks at top. With smaller needles, pick up and knit 70 (78, 86, 94, 102) sts across blocks.

Knit 3 rows.

Row 1: K2, *p2, k2; rep from * across.

Row 2: P2, *k2, p2; rep from * across.

Rep Rows 1 and 2 until ribbing measures 3 inches.

Bind off loosely in pat.

Front

Center Cable Panel

With larger needles cast on 18 sts. Work Rows 1–8 of Cable Panel pat for 88 (96, 102, 112, 120) rows.

Bind off loosely.

First Block

Row 1 (RS): Cast on 23 (25, 27, 29, 31) sts, with RS of Cable Panel facing, pick up and knit 22 (24, 26, 28, 30) sts along one side of Cable Panel, picking up at a rate of 3 sts for every 4 rows—45 (49, 53, 57, 61) sts.

Beg with Row 2, work as for First Block of back.

Second Block

Row 1 (RS): Pick up and knit 22 (24, 26, 28, 30) sts in ends of rows of previous block, pick up and knit 22 (24, 26, 28, 30) sts along side of Cable Panel, picking up sts as before—45 (49, 53, 57, 61) sts (includes st left on needle from previous block).

Beg with Row 2, work same as for First Block of back.

Third Block

Work same as for Second Block.

Work a second row of blocks in same manner as for back.

Turn Cable Panel and work 2 rows of blocks in same manner along opposite side.

Yoke

With larger needles and RS facing pick up and knit 95 (103, 113, 121, 129) sts across ends of rows of blocks and cable panel.

Knit 3 rows.

Work in St st until piece measures 21 (22, 23, 24, 25) inches, ending with a WS row.

Shape neck

Work 37 (40, 43, 46, 49) sts, place center 21 (23, 27, 29, 31) sts on a holder, attach a 2nd ball of yarn, work rem 37 (40, 43, 46, 49) sts.

Working both sides at once, continue in St st dec 1 st each side of neck edge [every row] 7 times—30 (33, 36, 39, 42) sts.

Work even until piece measures 24 (25, 26, 27, 28) inches.

Front Ribbing

With RS facing and smaller needles, pick up and knit 78 (86, 94, 102, 110) sts across opposite edge of blocks and cable panel.

Knit 3 rows.

Row 1: K2, *p2, k2; rep from * across.

Row 2: P2, *k2, p2; rep from * across.

Rep Rows 1 and 2 until ribbing measures 3 inches.

Bind off loosely in pat.

Assembly

Join shoulders using 3-Needle Bind-Off as follows: Place shoulder sts from the front on one needle and

place shoulders sts from back on another needle. Place front and back with RS tog and needles aligned in the same direction. With a third needle, knit one st from each needle tog, bind off at the same time.

Sleeves

Measure 9½ (10, 10½, 11, 11½) inches from shoulder seam on front and back, place markers. With RS facing and larger needles, pick up and knit 86 (90, 94, 98, 102) sts from marker to marker.

Knit 3 rows.

Work in St st dec 1 st each side [every 6th row] 10 times, then [every 4th row] 10 times—46 (50, 54, 58, 62) sts.

Work even until sleeve measures 18 inches, ending with a WS row.

Change to smaller needles.

Next row: Knit, dec 4 (4, 8, 8, 12) sts evenly spaced across—42 (46, 46, 50, 50 sts)

Knit 3 rows.

Next row: K2, *p2, k2; rep across.

Next row: P2, *k2, p2; rep across.

Rep last 2 rows until ribbing measures 3 inches.

Bind off loosely in pat.

Neckband

With RS facing and smaller circular needles, beg at one shoulder seam, pick up and knit 80 (84, 88, 92, 96) sts around neck opening including sts on holders. Join, placing marker on needle to mark beg of rnd.

Rnd 1: Purl.

Rnd 2: Knit.

Rnd 3: Purl.

Rnd 4–17: *K2, p2; rep from * around.

Bind off loosely in pat.

Finishing

Fold neckband in half to inside and sew in place.

Sew side and sleeve seams. ❖

Fourth Block	First Block	Cable Panel	Third Block	Sixth Block
Fifth Block	Second Block		Second Block	Fifth Block
Sixth Block	Third Block		First Block	Fourth Block

Front Block Diagram

Third Block	Sixth Block	Ninth Block	Twelfth Block
Second Block	Fifth Block	Eighth Block	Eleventh Block
First Block	Fourth Block	Seventh Block	Tenth Block

Back Block Diagram

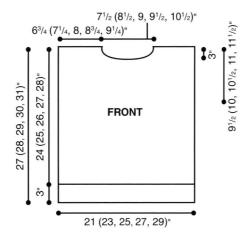

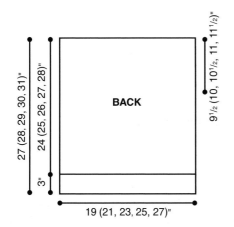

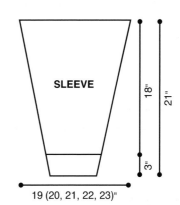

Extra-Fine Cardigan

Design by Andra Knight-Bowman

Skill Level

■■■□ INTERMEDIATE

Sizes

Woman's small (medium, large, extra-large, 2X-large) Instructions are given for smallest size, with larger sizes in parentheses. When only 1 number is given, it applies to all sizes.

Finished Measurements

Chest: 36 (40, 44, 48, 52) inches
Length: 21 (23, 25, 27, 29) inches

Materials

- Plymouth Trabajos del Peru 100% extra-fine merino wool worsted weight yarn (147 yds/100g per skein): 8 (9, 10, 11, 12) skeins variegated #11
- Size 9 (5.25mm) needles or size needed to obtain gauge
- Stitch holders
- Stitch markers
- 6 (¾-inch) buttons
- Tapestry needles

4 MEDIUM

Gauge

16 sts and 32 rows = 4 inches/10 cm in garter st. To save time, take time to check gauge.

Pattern Notes

Use thumb method cast-on as shown on page 4 for entire project.

Back and Front are worked by knitting the ribbing first and then working blocks in vertical rows from ribbing to shoulder (see block diagrams on page 27).

Back

Ribbing

Cast on 68 (76, 84, 92, 100) sts.

Row 1: *K2, p2; rep from * across.

Rep Row 1 until ribbing measures 3 inches.

Next row (RS): Knit 1 row.

Body

First Block

Row 1 (RS): Cast on 18 (20, 22, 24, 26) sts at end of needle. Turn.

Note: On following row k3tog is worked with cast-on and ribbing sts. At end of row, place rem unused ribbing sts on holder.

Row 2 (WS): K16 (18, 20, 22, 24), k3tog, k16 (18, 20, 22, 24) sts—33 (37, 41, 45, 49) sts.

Row 3 and all odd-numbered rows (RS): Knit.

Row 4: K15 (17, 19, 21, 23), k3tog, k15 (17, 19, 21, 23) sts.

Row 6: K14 (16, 18, 20, 22), k3tog, k14 (16, 18, 20, 22) sts.

Continue in this manner having 1 less st each side of the dec until 3 sts rem.

Next row: K3tog—1 st remains on needle. Do not finish off.

Second Block

Row 1 (RS): With RS of facing, pick up and knit 16 (18, 20, 22, 24) sts in ends of rows along side of previous block, cast on 18 (20, 22, 24, 26) sts—35 (39, 43, 47, 51) sts (includes st on needle at end of previous block).

Beg with Row 2 work same as for First Block.

Third and Fourth Blocks

Work same as for Second Block.

At end of Fourth Block, finish off.

Fifth Block

Row 1 (RS): With RS facing, attach yarn in bottom right-hand corner of First Block, pick up and knit 18 (20, 22, 24, 26) sts in ends of rows along the side of block. Turn.

Beg with Row 2 work same as for First Block, working across picked-up sts and ribbing sts from holder.

Sixth Block

Row 1 (RS): With RS of facing, pick up and knit 16 (18, 20, 22, 24) sts in ends of rows along side of previous block, pick up and knit 18 (20, 22, 24, 26) sts in ends of rows along edge of corresponding block in previous row—35 (39, 43, 47, 51) sts (includes st on needle at end of previous block).

Beg with Row 2 work same as for First Block.

Continue adding blocks in this manner until there 4 rows of 4 blocks each.

Fasten off.

Right Front

Ribbing

Cast on 40 (44, 48, 52, 56) sts.

Row 1 (WS): *K2, p2; rep from * to last 4 sts, k2, p1, k1.

Row 2 (RS): *K2, p2; rep from * across.

Rows 3 and 4: Rep Rows 1 and 2.

Row 5: Rep Row 1.

Row 6 (buttonhole row): K2, p2tog, yo, *k2, p2; rep from * across.

Rep Rows 1 and 2 until ribbing measures 3 inches.

Next row: K2, p2, k2, knit to end of row.

Body

Cast on 18 (20, 22, 24, 26) sts at end of needle. Work as for back making 2 rows with 4 blocks in each row. Place rem 6 sts on a holder for band. Fasten off.

Right Front Band

Place sts from holder on needle and attach yarn.

Row 1 (RS): K2, p2, k1, knit in front and back of next st—7 sts.

Row 2: P3, k2, p1, k1.

Row 3: K2, p2, k3.

Rep Rows 2 and 3 until band measures 17 (18, 19, 20, 21) inches, *at the same time,* create a buttonhole as before [every 20 (22, 24, 26, 28) rows] 5 times. Place sts on holder.

House of White Birches, Berne, Indiana 46711

Body

Cast on 18 (20, 22, 24, 26) sts at end of needle. Turn.

Work as for back, having 2 rows with 4 blocks in each row. Fasten off.

Left Front Band

Place sts from holder on a needle and attach yarn.

Row 1 (RS): Knit in front and back of first st, k1, p2, k2—7 sts.

Row 2: K1, p1, k2, p3.

Row 3: K3, p2, k2.

Rep Rows 2 and 3 until band measures 17 (18, 19, 20, 21) inches. Place sts on a holder.

Assembly

Sew rib bands to fronts.

With RS of front and back tog, sew armhole edge blocks tog for shoulder.

Neckband

With RS facing, beg at center right front, slip sts for right front band from holder to LH needle, attach yarn, k2, p2, k1, k2tog; pick up and knit 62 (66, 70, 74, 78) st across right front block, 2 back blocks and left front block; slip the 7 sts for left front band from holder to LH needle, k2tog, k1, p2, k2—74 (78, 82, 86, 90) sts.

Row 1 (WS): K1, p1 *k2, p2; rep from * to last 4 sts, k2, p1, k1.

Row 2 (RS): *K2, p2; rep from * to last 2 sts, k2.

Rep Rows 1 and 2 until neck band measure 3 inches.

Bind off loosely in pat.

Sleeves

Measure 8 (8½, 9, 9½, 10) inches from shoulder and place marker at armhole edge on each side of front and back. With RS facing pick up and knit 68 (72, 76, 80, 84) sts evenly spaced between marker. Do not join, work back and forth in rows.

Row 1: *K2, p2; rep from * across.

Rep Row 1 until sleeve measures 7 inches.

Continue in rib pat as established dec 1 st each end [every 4th row] 16 times.

Work even until sleeve measures 19½ (20, 20, 20, 20) inches.

Bind off loosely in pat.

Left Front

Ribbing

Cast on 40 (44, 48, 52, 56) sts.

Row 1 (WS): K1, p1, *k2, p2; rep from * to last 2 sts, k2.

Row 2 (RS): *P2, k2; rep from * across.

Rep Rows 1 and 2 until ribbing measures 3 inches.

Next row: Knit to last 6 sts and place them on a holder.

Finishing

Sew side and sleeve seams, reversing seam for last 2 inches for fold back cuff.

Sew button on left front band opposite buttonholes. ❖

Fourth Block	Eighth Block
Third Block	Seventh Block
Second Block	Sixth Block
First Block	Fifth Block

Front Block Diagram

Fourth Block	Eighth Block	Twelfth Block	Sixteenth Block
Third Block	Seventh Block	Eleventh Block	Fifteenth Block
Second Block	Sixth Block	Tenth Block	Fourteenth Block
First Block	Fifth Block	Ninth Block	Thirteenth Block

Back Block Diagram

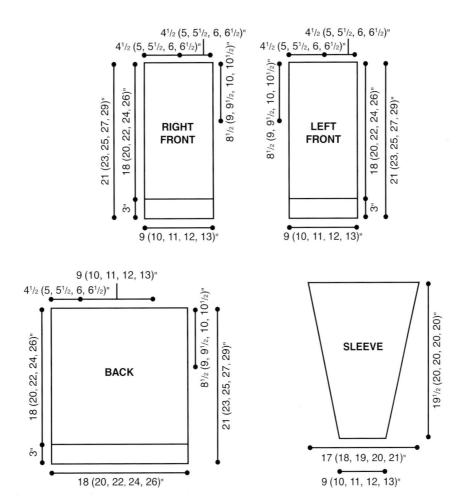

Midnight Hoodie Vest

Design by Andra Knight-Bowman

Skill Level

 ■■■□ INTERMEDIATE

Sizes

Woman's small (medium, large, extra-large, 2X-large) Instructions are given for smallest size, with larger sizes in parentheses. When only 1 number is given, it applies to all sizes.

Finished Measurements

Width: 36 (40, 44, 48, 52) inches
Length: 19 (21, 23, 25, 26) inches

Materials

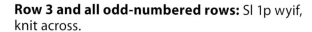

- Berroco Jasper 100% fine merino wool worsted weight yarn (98 yds/50g per hank): 8 (9, 10, 11, 12) hanks black galaxy #3823
- Size 9 (5.25mm) needles or size needed to obtain gauge
- Spare needle for joining hoodie seam
- Tapestry needle
- Stitch markers
- 1 (2-inch) square button

Gauge

16 sts and 32 row = 4 inches/10 cm in garter st. To save time, take time to check gauge.

Pattern Notes

Use thumb method cast-on as shown on page 4 for entire project.

Vest is made in 4 pieces to create mirror image blocks. Back is seamed down the middle.

Slip first stitch of every row purlwise with yarn in front then take yarn to back between needles.

Left Back

Body Block

Cast on 71 (79, 87, 95, 103) sts.

Row 1 (RS): Sl 1p wyif, knit across. Mark as RS.

Row 2: Sl 1p wyif, k33 (37, 41, 45, 49), k3tog, k34, (38, 42, 46, 50).

Row 3 and all odd-numbered rows: Sl 1p wyif, knit across.

Row 4: Sl 1p wyif, k32, (36, 40, 44, 48), k3tog, k33 (37, 41, 45, 49).

Continue to work in this manner, having 1 less st on each side of dec until 3 sts rem.

Next row: K3tog—1 st remains on needle. Do not finish off.

Yoke Block

Row 1 (RS): With RS facing, working in sl sts across edge of previous block, pick up and knit 28 (32, 36, 40, 40) sts, leaving 6 (6, 6, 6, 12) ridges unworked for armhole; cast on 30 (34, 38, 42, 42) sts—59 (67, 75, 83, 83) sts on needle (includes st on needle at end of previous block).

Row 2: Sl 1p wyif, k27 (31, 35, 39, 39), k3tog, k28 (32, 36, 40, 40) sts.

Row 3 and all odd-numbered rows: Sl 1p wyif, knit across.

Row 4: Sl 1p wyif, k 26 (30, 34, 38, 38), k3tog, k27 (31, 35, 39, 39) sts.

Continue to work in this manner, having 1 st less on each side of dec until 3 sts rem.

Next row: K3tog. Fasten off.

Right Back

Body Block

Work same as Body Block for Left Back. Fasten off.

Yoke Block

Row 1(RS): With RS facing, turn block one-quarter turn to the left, placing cast-on edge at right and bottom of block and creating a mirror image of left back. Cast on 30 (34, 38, 42, 42) sts, leaving 6 (6, 6, 6, 12) ridges unworked for armhole, pick up and knit 29 (33, 37, 41, 41) sts across top of previous block—59, 67, 75, 83, 83 sts on needle.

Row 2: Sl 1p wyif, k27 (31, 35, 39, 39), k3tog, k28 (32, 36, 40, 40) sts.

Row 3 and all odd-numbered rows: Sl 1p wyif, knit across.

Row 4: Sl 1p wyif, k26 (30, 34, 38, 38), k3tog, k27 (31, 35, 39, 39).

Continue to work in this manner, having 1 st less on each side of dec until 3 sts rem.

Next row: K3tog. Fasten off. Sew 2 back pieces tog, with seam at center back.

Right Front
Work as for Left Back through Row 4 of Yoke Block.

Next row (buttonhole row): Sl 1p wyif, k2, bind off next 2 sts, complete row.

Next row: Continue in pat, casting on 2 sts over 2 bound-off sts.

Complete as for left back. Fasten off.

Left Front
Work as for Right Back.

Assembly
Sew Left and Right back tog at center back.

Sew fronts and back tog for 3½ (4, 4½, 5, 5) inches for each shoulder.

Sew side seams.

Hoodie
With RS facing, join yarn at center right front neck edge, pick up and knit 1 st in each sl st across right front, back and left front adjusting as necessary to have an even number of sts.

Next row: Sl 1p wyif, knit across. Mark center of row.

Continuing to sl first st, work even in garter st until hood measures 11 inches, ending with a WS row.

Next row: Sl 1p wyif, knit to 2 sts before marker, k2tog, slip marker, ssk, knit to end.

Next row: Sl 1p wyif, knit across.

Rep [last 2 rows] twice.

Join hood: Work to marker, place sts with RS tog, having needles aligned in the same direction. Knit 1 st from each needle tog, binding them off at the same time.

Bottom Borders
With RS facing, pick up and knit 1 st in each st across back.

Row 1: Sl 1p wyif, knit across.

Rep Row 1 until border measures 3 inches.

Bind off loosely.

Rep for left and right front borders.

Sew button opposite buttonhole. ❖

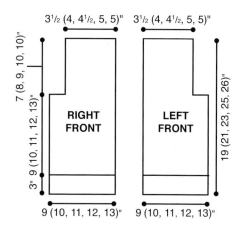

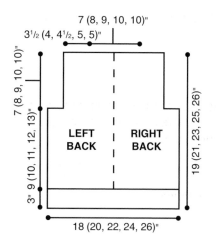

Winter Sky Hoodie

Design by Andra Knight-Bowman

Skill Level

■■■□ INTERMEDIATE

Sizes

Woman's small (medium, large, extra-large, 2X-large) Instructions are given for smallest size, with larger sizes in parentheses. When only 1 number is given, it applies to all sizes.

Finished Measurements

Width: 36 (40, 44, 48, 52) inches
Length: 19 (21, 23, 25, 26) inches

Materials

- Berroco Jasper 100% fine merino wool worsted weight yarn (98 yds/50g per hank): 8 (9, 10, 11, 12) hanks mochica blue #3844
- Size 9 (5.25mm) needles or size needed to obtain gauge
- Spare needle for joining hoodie seam
- Tapestry needle
- Stitch markers

Gauge

16 sts and 32 row = 4 inches/10 cm in garter st.
To save time, take time to check gauge.

Pattern Notes

Use thumb method cast-on as shown on page 4 for entire project.

The front/back of the sweater is made in 2 pieces to create mirror-image blocks and seamed down the middle

Slip first stitch of every row purlwise with yarn in front then take yarn to back between needles.

House of White Birches, Berne, Indiana 46711

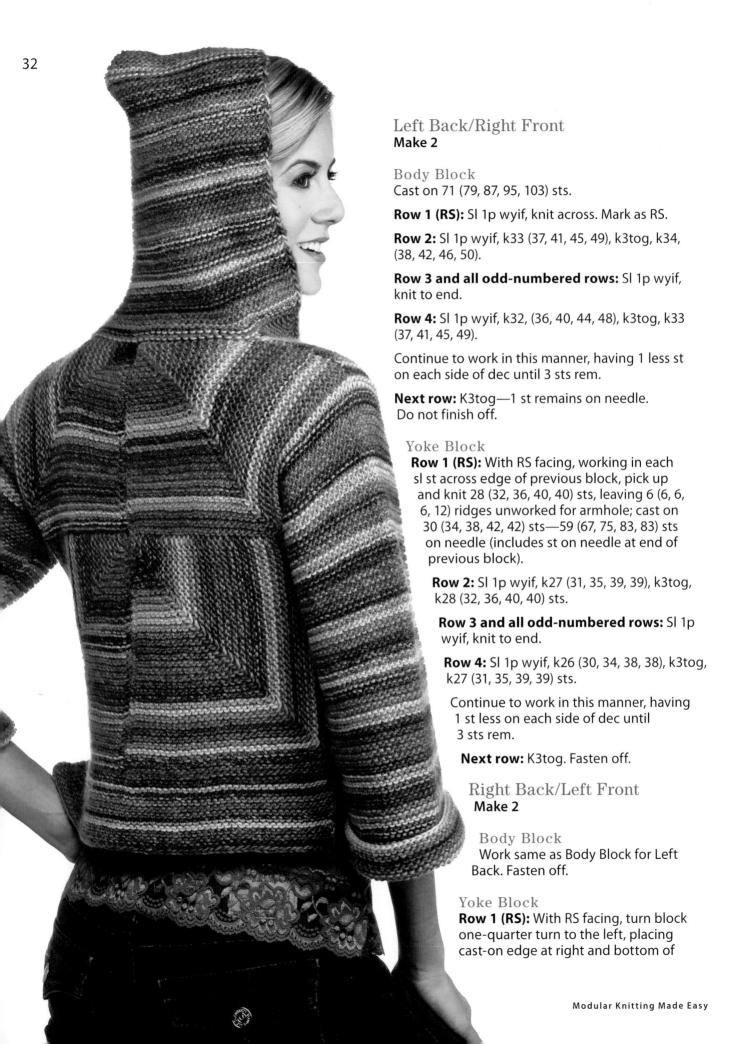

Left Back/Right Front
Make 2

Body Block
Cast on 71 (79, 87, 95, 103) sts.

Row 1 (RS): Sl 1p wyif, knit across. Mark as RS.

Row 2: Sl 1p wyif, k33 (37, 41, 45, 49), k3tog, k34, (38, 42, 46, 50).

Row 3 and all odd-numbered rows: Sl 1p wyif, knit to end.

Row 4: Sl 1p wyif, k32, (36, 40, 44, 48), k3tog, k33 (37, 41, 45, 49).

Continue to work in this manner, having 1 less st on each side of dec until 3 sts rem.

Next row: K3tog—1 st remains on needle. Do not finish off.

Yoke Block
Row 1 (RS): With RS facing, working in each sl st across edge of previous block, pick up and knit 28 (32, 36, 40, 40) sts, leaving 6 (6, 6, 6, 12) ridges unworked for armhole; cast on 30 (34, 38, 42, 42) sts—59 (67, 75, 83, 83) sts on needle (includes st on needle at end of previous block).

Row 2: Sl 1p wyif, k27 (31, 35, 39, 39), k3tog, k28 (32, 36, 40, 40) sts.

Row 3 and all odd-numbered rows: Sl 1p wyif, knit to end.

Row 4: Sl 1p wyif, k26 (30, 34, 38, 38), k3tog, k27 (31, 35, 39, 39) sts.

Continue to work in this manner, having 1 st less on each side of dec until 3 sts rem.

Next row: K3tog. Fasten off.

Right Back/Left Front
Make 2

Body Block
Work same as Body Block for Left Back. Fasten off.

Yoke Block
Row 1 (RS): With RS facing, turn block one-quarter turn to the left, placing cast-on edge at right and bottom of

block and creating a mirror image of left back. Cast on 30 (34, 38, 42, 42) sts, leaving first 6 (6, 6, 6, 12) ridges at top of block unworked for armhole, pick up and knit 29 (33, 37, 41, 41) sts—59 (67, 75, 83, 83) sts on needle.

Row 2: Sl 1p wyif, k27 (31, 35, 39, 39), k3tog, k28 (32, 36, 40, 40) sts.

Row 3 and all odd-numbered rows: Sl 1p wyif, knit across.

Row 4: Sl 1p wyif, k26 (30, 34, 38, 38), k3tog, k27 (31, 35, 39, 39).

Continue to work in this manner, having 1 st less on each side of dec until 3 sts rem.

Next row: K3tog. Fasten off.

Sew 2 back pieces tog with seam at center back.

Sew 2 front pieces tog with seam at center front, leaving 7½ (8, 8½, 9, 9) inches open at the neck edge for V-neck.

Sew fronts and back tog for 3½ (4, 4½, 5, 5) inches for each shoulder.

Hoodie
With RS Facing, join yarn at center right front neck edge, pick up and knit 1 st in each sl st across right front, back and left front, adjusting as necessary to have an even number of sts.

Next row: Sl 1p wyif, knit across. Mark center of row.

Continuing to sl first st, work even in garter st until hood measures 11 inches, ending with a WS row.

Next row: Sl 1p wyif, knit to 2 sts before marker, k2tog, slip marker, ssk, knit to end.

Next row: Sl 1p wyif, knit across.

Rep [last 2 rows] twice.

Join hood: Work to marker, place sts with RS tog, having needles aligned the same way. Knit 1 st from each needle tog, binding them off at the same time.

Sleeves
With RS facing, pick up and knit 60 (68, 76, 84, 84) sts along inset portion of sleeve (between A and B on Fig. 1).

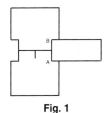

Fig. 1

Row 1: Sl 1p wyif, knit across.

Rep Row 1 until sleeve measures 18 (18, 19, 19, 19) inches.

Bind off loosely.

Sew top side edges of sleeve to armhole. Sew side and sleeve seams. Reverse seam for cuff, if desired.

Bottom Borders
With RS facing, pick up and knit 1 st in each st across back.

Row 1: Sl 1, knit across.

Rep Row 1 until border measures 3 inches.

Bind off loosely.

Rep across front. Leave sides of bottom border open. ❖

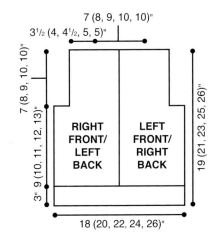

7 (8, 9, 10, 10)"

3½ (4, 4½, 5, 5)"

7 (8, 9, 10, 10)"

3" 9 (10, 11, 12, 13)"

RIGHT FRONT/ LEFT BACK

LEFT FRONT/ RIGHT BACK

19 (21, 23, 25, 26)"

18 (20, 22, 24, 26)"

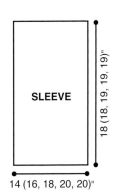

SLEEVE

18 (18, 19, 19, 19)"

14 (16, 18, 20, 20)"

House of White Birches, Berne, Indiana 46711   DRGnetwork.com

Long Luxurious Coat

Design by Andra Knight-Bowman

Skill Level
 INTERMEDIATE

Sizes
Woman's sizes small (medium, large, extra-large, 2X-large) Instructions are given for smallest size, with larger sizes in parentheses. When only 1 number is given, it applies to all sizes.

Finished Measurements
Chest: 38 (42, 46, 50, 54) inches
Length: 30 (31½, 34½, 37½, 40½) inches

Materials
- Plymouth King George 45% baby alpaca/45% merino wool/10% cashmere worsted weight yarn (105 yds/50g per ball): 17 (19, 21, 23, 25) balls off-white #100
- Size 7 (4.25mm) straight and 32-inch circular needles or size needed to obtain gauge
- Lock ring markers
- 7 (⅞-inch) buttons
- Tapestry needle

Gauge
18 sts and 24 rows = 4 inches/10 cm in St st. To save time, take time to check gauge.

Special Abbreviation
Central double decrease (CDD): Slip next 2 sts as if to k2tog, k1, pass 2 slipped stitches over.

Pattern Notes
Use thumb method cast-on as shown on page 4 for entire project.

Slip stitches knitwise if knitting and purlwise if purling.

Seed stitch border for back and front is worked first. Right Back/Left Front is worked in 2 vertical rows of blocks from lower border to shoulder (see block diagram on page 38). Left Back/Right Front is worked in 6 horizontal rows from lower border to shoulder (see block diagram) to create mirror image blocks. Back is worked in two pieces to create mirror image blocks then seamed in the middle.

Pattern Stitch
Seed Stitch Pattern

Row 1: *K1, p1; rep from * across.

Row 2: Knit the purl sts, purl the knit sts.

Rep Row 2 for pat.

Right Back/Left Front
Make 2

Border
Cast on 40 (44, 48, 52, 56) sts. Work in seed st for 13 rows.

Knit 1 row.

Body
Row 1

First Block
Row 1 (RS): Cast on 21 (23, 25, 27, 29) sts at end of needle.

Row 2: Sl 1p, purl 40 (44, 48, 52, 56) sts—41 (45, 49, 53, 57) sts.

Place rem sts of seed st border on separate needle or holder.

Row 3: Sl 1k, k18 (20, 22, 24, 26), CDD, k19 (21, 23, 25, 27) sts.

Row 4 and all even numbered rows: Sl 1p, purl across.

Row 5: Sl 1k, k17 (19, 21, 23, 25), CDD, k18 (20, 22, 24, 26) sts.

Row 7: Sl 1k, k16 (18, 20, 22, 24), CDD, k17 (19, 21, 23, 25) sts.

Continue in this manner, having 1 less st on each of dec until 3 sts rem.

Next row: CDD—1 st remains on needle. Do not finish off.

Second Block
With RS facing, pick up and knit 19 (21, 23, 25, 27) in ends of rows along edge of previous block, cast on

21 (23, 25, 27, 29) sts. Turn. Sl 1p, purl across—41 (45, 49, 53, 57) sts (includes st on needle at end of previous block).

Beg with Row 3, work same as for First Block.

Third through Sixth Blocks
Rep Second Block until there are 6 blocks in the row. Fasten off at end of last block.

Row 2

Seventh Block
With RS facing and beg in bottom right-hand corner of First Block, pick up and knit 21 (23, 25, 27, 29) sts in ends of rows along side of block. Turn. Sl 1p, purl 40 (44, 48, 52, 56) sts—41 (45, 49, 53, 57) sts (includes rem border sts).

Beg with Row 3, work same as First Block.

Additional Blocks
With RS facing, pick up and knit 19 (21, 23, 25, 27) in ends of rows of previous block, pick up and knit 21 (23, 25, 27, 29) sts in ends of rows of corresponding block in previous row. Turn. Sl 1p, purl across—41 (45, 49, 53, 57) sts (includes st on needle at end of previous block).

Beg with Row 3, work same as for First Block.

At end of last block, fasten off.

Left Back/Right Front
Make 2

Border
Cast on 40 (44, 48, 52, 56) sts. Work in seed st for 13 rows.

Body

Row 1

First Block
Cast on 21 (23, 25, 27, 29) sts at end of needle.

Row 1 (RS): Sl 1k, k40 (43, 47, 51, 55) sts—41 (45, 49, 53, 57) sts. Place rem sts of border on separate needle or holder.

Row 2: Sl 1p, purl across.

Beg with Row 3, complete as for First Block of Right Back/Left Front.

Note: The Left Back/Right Front blocks form a mirror image of the Right Back/Left Front blocks and are worked in 6 horizontal rows of 2 blocks each.

Second Block

With RS facing pick up and knit 20 (22, 24, 26, 28) sts in ends of rows of previous block, k20 (22, 24, 26, 28) sts from holder. Turn. Sl 1p, purl across—41 (45, 49, 53, 57) sts (includes st on needle at end of previous block).

Beg with Row 3, complete as for First Block of Right Back/Left Front. Fasten off.

Row 2

First Block

Cast on 21 (23, 25, 27, 29), pick up and knit 20 (22, 24, 26, 28) sts in ends of rows along side of corresponding block in previous row. Turn. Sl 1, purl across—41 (45, 49, 53, 57) sts.

Beg with Row 3, work same as for First Block of Right Back/Left Front.

Second Block

With RS facing, pick up and knit 19 (21, 23, 25, 27) in ends of rows of previous block, pick up and knit 21 (23, 25, 27, 29) sts in ends of rows of corresponding block in previous row. Turn. Sl 1p, purl across—41 (45, 49, 53, 57) sts (includes st on needle at end of previous block).

Work same as for First Block of Right Back/Left Front. Fasten off.

Additional Rows

Continue in this manner until there are a total of 12 blocks in 6 rows with 2 blocks in each row. Fasten off.

Assembly

Sew Right Back and Left Back tog at center back.

Left Front Band

Hold Left Front with RS facing, beg at top (neck edge) with circular needle, pick up and knit 20 (22, 24, 26, 28) sts in each block and 7 sts in seed st border—127 (139, 151, 163, 175) sts.

Work in seed st for 13 rows. Bind off loosely in pat.

Right Front Band

Hold Right Front with RS facing, beg at lower edge with circular needles, starting at bottom of right side, pick up and knit 7 sts in seed st band and 20 (22, 24, 26, 28) sts in each block—127 (139, 151, 163, 175) sts.

Work in seed st for 5 rows.

Next row (buttonhole row): Continuing in pat as established, work 2 sts, *k2tog, yo, work in pat across 18 (20, 22, 24, 26) sts; rep from * 6 times, k2tog, yo, k3.

Continue is seed st for 7 more rows. Bind off loosely in pat.

Place fronts and back with RS tog. Sew block at armhole edge tog for shoulder, leaving center blocks for collar.

Collar

With WS facing and beg with left front, pick up and knit 7 sts across end of left front band, pick up and knit 20 (22, 24, 26, 28) in each block around neck edge, pick up and knit 7 sts across end of right front band.

Work 4 rows in seed st.

Continue in seed st inc 1 st at each end of next row, then [every 4th row] 7 times, working additional sts into pat.

Work 4 more rows in seed st. Bind off loosely in pat.

Sleeves

Measure 8¼ (9, 9½, 10¼, 10¾) inches from shoulder seam along armhole edge of front and back, place markers for sleeve opening.

With RS facing, pick up and knit 74 (80, 86, 92, 98) sts between markers.

Work in St st, dec 1 st each side [every 10th row] 9 times—56 (62, 68, 74, 80) sts.

Work even until sleeve measures 16 inches.

Work in seed st for 13 rows. Bind off loosely in pat.

Left Pocket

Measure 15½ inches from shoulder seam on back and front on left side edge and place marker for pocket placement.

With RS of back facing, pick up 32 sts along edge of back beg at marker.

Work in St st for 13 inches. Bind off.

Sew bound-off edge to left front matching placement with back.

With RS facing and left front, starting where pocket was sewn, pick up and 32 sts for pocket trim. Work 7 rows in Seed st. Bind off loosely in pat.

Right Pocket

Measure 22½ inches from shoulder seam on back and front on right side edge and place marker for pocket placement.

With RS of back facing, pick up 32 sts along edge of back beg at marker.

Work in St st for 13 inches. Bind off.

Sew bound-off edge to right front matching placement with back.

With RS facing and right front, starting where pocket was sewn, pick up and 32 sts for pocket trim.

Work 7 rows in Seed st. Bind off loosely in pat.

Finishing
Sew sides of pocket tog and tack each corner to front to hold in place.

Sew sleeve and side seams, omitting the pocket area. ❖

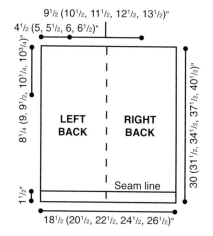

Left Back / Right Front Block Diagram

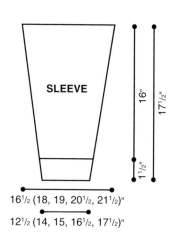

Right Back / Left Front Block Diagram

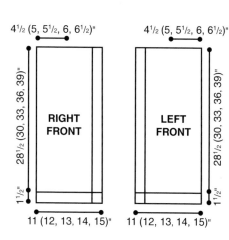

Royal Silk Turtleneck

Design by Andra Knight-Bowman

Skill Level

■■■□ INTERMEDIATE

Sizes

Woman's small (medium, large, extra-large, 2X-large)
Instructions are given for smallest size, with larger
sizes in parentheses. When only 1 number is given,
it applies to all sizes.

Finished Measurements

Chest: 36 (40, 44, 48, 52) inches
Length: 21 (23, 25, 27, 29) inches

Materials

- Plymouth Royal Llama Silk 60% fine
  llama/40% silk worsted weight yarn
  (102 yds/50g per skein): 9 (10, 11, 12, 13) skeins
  blue/gray mix #1837
- Size 7 (4.5mm) straight and 16-inch
  circular needles
- Size 9 (5.25mm) straight needles or size
  needed to obtain gauge
- Tapestry needle
- Stitch markers

Gauge

16 sts and 32 rows = 4 inches/10 cm in garter st on
larger needles.
To save time, take time to check gauge.

Pattern Notes

Use thumb method cast-on as shown on page 4
for entire project.

Back and Front are worked by knitting the ribbing
first and then working blocks in vertical rows from
side-to-side (see block diagram on page 40).

Back/Front

With smaller needles cast on 68 (76, 84, 92, 100) sts.

Ribbing

Row 1: *K2, p2; rep from * across.

Rep Row 1 until ribbing measures 3 inches.

Next row (RS): Knit 1 row.

Body

Row 1

First Block

Row 1 (RS): Cast on 18 (20, 22, 24, 26) sts at end
of needle.

Change to larger needles.

*Note: On following row k3tog is worked with cast-on
and ribbing sts. At end of row, place rem unused
ribbing sts on holder or leave on smaller needle.*

Row 2 (WS): K16 (18, 20, 22, 24), k3tog, k16 (18, 20, 22, 24) sts.

Row 3 and all odd-numbered rows (RS): Knit.

Row 4: K15 (17, 19, 21, 23), k3tog, k15 (17, 19, 21, 23) sts.

Continue in this manner having 1 less st each side of the dec until 3 sts rem.

Next row: K3tog—1 st remains on needle. Do not finish off.

Second Block

Row 1 (RS): With RS of facing and larger needles, pick up and knit 16 (18, 20, 22, 24) sts in ends of rows along edge of previous block, cast on 18 (20, 22, 24, 26) sts—35 (39, 43, 47, 51) sts (includes st on needle at end of previous block).

Beg with Row 2 work same as for First Block.

Third and Fourth Blocks

Work same as for Second Block.

At end of Fourth Block, finish off.

Row 2

Fifth Block

Row 1 (RS): With RS facing, attach yarn in bottom right-hand corner of First Block, pick up and knit 18 (20, 22, 24, 26) sts in ends of rows along the side. Turn.

Beg with Row 2 work same as for First Block working across picked-up sts and ribbing sts.

Sixth Block

Row 1 (RS): With RS of facing, pick up and knit 16 (18, 20, 22, 24) sts in ends of rows along side of previous block, pick up and knit 18 (20, 22, 24, 26) sts in ends of rows along side of corresponding block in previous row—35 (39, 43, 47, 51) sts (includes st on needle at end of previous block).

Beg with Row 2 work same as for First Block.

Continue adding blocks in this manner until there
4 rows of 4 blocks each. Fasten off.

Assembly

Place front and back with RS tog. Sew outer armhole edge blocks tog for shoulder.

Neckband

With RS facing and circular needle, beg at a shoulder seam, pick up and knit 76 (80, 84, 88, 92) sts evenly spaced across 2 center blocks of front and back. Join, placing marker at beg of rnd.

Rnd 1: *K2, p2; rep from * around.

Rep Rnd 1 until ribbing measures 7 inches.

Bind off loosely in pat.

Sleeves

Measure 8 (8½, 9, 9½, 10) inches from shoulder and place marker on each side of front and back. With RS facing and larger needles pick up and knit 68 (72, 76, 80, 84) sts evenly spaced between marker. Do not join, work back and forth in rows.

Row 1: *K2, p2; rep from * across.

Rep Row 1 until sleeve measures 7 inches.

Continue in rib pat as established dec 1 st each end [every 4th row] 16 times.

Work even until sleeve measures 19½ (20, 20, 20, 20) inches.

Bind off loosely in pat.

Finishing

Sew side and sleeve seams, reversing seam for last 2 inches for fold back cuff. ❖

Fourth Block	Eighth Block	Twelfth Block	Sixteenth Block
Third Block	Seventh Block	Eleventh Block	Fifteenth Block
Second Block	Sixth Block	Tenth Block	Fourteenth Block
First Block	Fifth Block	Ninth Block	Thirteenth Block

Front/Back Block Diagram

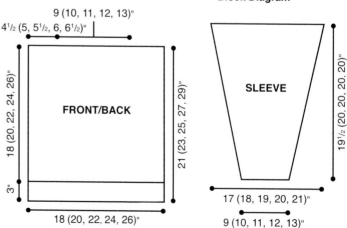

9 (10, 11, 12, 13)"
4½ (5, 5½, 6, 6½)"

18 (20, 22, 24, 26)"

FRONT/BACK

21 (23, 25, 27, 29)"

3"

18 (20, 22, 24, 26)"

SLEEVE

19½ (20, 20, 20, 20)"

17 (18, 19, 20, 21)"

9 (10, 11, 12, 13)"

Smart & Sassy Dog Sweater

Design by Andra Knight-Bowman

Skill level

 INTERMEDIATE

Finished Measurements

Width: 9 inches
Length: 12 inches

Materials

- Plymouth Encore Worsted 75% acrylic/25% wool worsted weight yarn (200 yds/100g per ball): 1 ball red #1386
- Size 8 (5mm) needles or size needed to obtain gauge
- Cable needle
- Tapestry needle
- 2 (¾-inch) buttons

Gauge

18 sts and 36 rows = 4 inches/10cm in garter st. To save time, take time to check gauge.

Special Abbreviations

Cable front (CF): Slip next 4 sts on cable needle, hold in front, k4, k4 from cable needle.

Cable back (CB): Slip next 4 sts on cable needle, hold in back, k4, k4 from cable needle.

Pattern Stitch

Cable Panel Pattern (worked over 18 sts)

Row 1 (RS): K1, p2, k12, p2, k1.

Row 2: P1, k2, p12, k2, p1.

Row 3: K1, p2, CF, k4, p2, k1.

Row 4: Rep Row 2.

Rows 5 and 6: Rep Rows 1 and 2.

Row 7: K1, p2, k4, CB, p2, k1.

Row 8: P1, k2, p12, k2, p1.

Rep Rows 1–8 for pat.

Pattern Notes

Use thumb method cast-on as shown on page 4 for entire project.

Coat is made by working center cable panel first then picking up stitches along each side of the panel for the modular blocks.

Dog Coat

Cast on 18 sts.

Work Cable Panel pat for 60 rows.

Bind off loosely.

First Block

Cast on 16 sts, with RS of Cable Panel facing, pick up and knit 15 sts along one side of cable panel at the rate of 3 sts for every 4 rows—31 sts. Turn.

Row 1 (WS): K14, k3tog, k14.

Row 2 (RS) and all even-numbered rows: Knit.

Row 3: K13, k3tog, k13.

Row 5: K12, k3tog, k12.

Row 7: K11, k3tog, k11.

Row 9: K10, k3tog, k10.

Row 11: K9, k3tog, k9.

Row 13: K8, k3tog, k8.

Row 15: K7, k3tog, k7.

Row 17: K6, k3tog, k6.

Row 19: K5, k3tog, k5.

Row 21: K4, k3tog, k4.

Row 23: K3, k3tog, k3.

Row 25: K2, k3tog, k2.

Row 27: K1, k3tog, k1.

Row 29: K3tog—1 st remains on needle. Do not finish off.

Second Block

With RS of previous block facing, pick up and knit 15 sts in ends of rows along edge previous block, pick up and knit 15 sts along cable panel as before—31 sts (includes st on needle from previous block).

Work as for Rows 1–29 of First Block.

Third Block

Work as for Second Block. Fasten off.

Rep First, Second and Third Blocks on opposite side of Cable Panel. Do not fasten off at end of Third Block.

Bottom border

With RS facing, pick up and knit 47 sts in ends of rows of blocks and cable—48 sts (includes st on needle from previous block).

Knit 7 rows.

Bind off.

Collar

Hold piece with opposite edge of cable facing, pick up and knit 48 sts across in ends of rows of blocks and cable, cast on 5 sts—53 sts.

Knit 3 rows.

Next Row (buttonhole row): Knit to last 4 sts, yo, k2tog, k2.

Knit 3 rows.

Bind off loosely.

Side band

Cast on 30 sts.

Knit 3 rows.

Next Row (buttonhole row): Knit to last 4 sts, yo, k2tog, k2.

Knit 3 rows.

Bind off loosely.

Finishing

Referring to photo for placement, sew side band at the top of the middle block on the same side as collar tab.

Sew buttons opposite buttonholes. ❖

Baby Blocks Blanket

Design by Andra Knight-Bowman

Skill Level

 INTERMEDIATE

Finished Measurements

Approx 33 x 33 inches

Materials

- Plymouth Dreambaby Shine 45% microfiber acrylic/45% nylon/10% rayon DK weight yarn (160 yds/50g per ball): 2 balls each yellow #101 (A), blue #102 (B), white #100 (C), green #105 (D) and pink #119 (E)
- Size 6 (4.25mm) needle or size needed to obtain gauge

Gauge

21 sts and 42 rows = 4 inches/10 cm in garter st.

To save time, take time to check gauge.

Pattern Notes

Use thumb method cast-on as shown on page 4 for entire project.

Refer to chart for block color.

It is helpful to mark right side of first block with a small pin or scrap of a different color yarn.

Blanket

Row 1

First Block

With color A, cast on 65 sts.

Row 1 and all odd-numbered rows (RS): Knit.

Row 2 (WS): K31, k3tog, k31.

Row 4: K30, k3tog, k30.

Row 6: K29, k3tog, k29.

Row 8: K28, k3tog, k28.

Row 10: K27, k3tog, k27.

Continue in this manner having 1 less st on each side of k3tog dec until 3 sts remain.

Last Row: K3tog—1 st remains on needle. Do not fasten off. Turn.

Second Block

Row 1 (RS): With RS facing and B, pick up and knit 31 sts in ends of rows along edge of First Block, cast on 33 sts—65 sts (includes st on needle at end of previous block).

Beg with Row 2 work same as for First Block.

Third through Fifth Blocks

Work same as Second Block working colors as shown on chart. At end of Fifth Block, fasten off.

Row 2

First Block

Row 1 (RS): With B, cast on 32 sts, with RS of First Block on Row 1 facing, pick up and knit 33 sts in ends of rows along edge—65 sts.

Beg with Row 2 work same as for First Block on Row 1.

Second Block

Row 1 (RS): With RS facing and C, pick up and knit 31 sts in ends of rows along edge of previous block on same row, pick up and knit 33 sts in ends of rows along top edge of corresponding block on previous row—65 sts (includes st on needle at end of previous block).

Beg with Row 2 work same as for First Block on Row 1.

Third through Fifth Blocks

Work same as for Second Block working colors as shown on chart. At end of Fifth Block, fasten off.

Rows 3 through 5

Following chart, for color sequence, work in same manner as for Row 2 until all 25 blocks are complete.

Left Border

Hold piece with RS of left edge facing. With D, pick up and knit 32 sts in each block across—160 sts.

Knit 9 rows. Bind off loosely.

Right Border

Hold piece with RS facing of right edge facing. With A, pick up and knit 32 sts in each block across—160 sts.

Knit 9 rows. Bind off loosely.

Top Border

Hold piece with RS facing of top edge facing. With C, pick up and knit 6 sts across border, with B pick up and knit 32 sts in each block across, with C, pick up and knit 6 sts across border.

Knit 9 rows bringing new color under previous color to twist yarn on WS of work.

Bind off loosely.

Bottom Border

Hold piece with RS of bottom facing. With C, pick up and knit 6 sts across border, with E pick up and knit 32 sts in each block across, with C, pick up and knit 6 sts across border.

Knit 9 rows bringing new color under previous color to twist yarn on WS of work.

Bind off loosely. ❖

COLOR KEY
- ☐ Yellow
- ☐ Blue
- ☐ White
- ☐ Green
- ☐ Pink

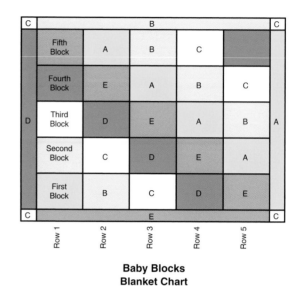

**Baby Blocks
Blanket Chart**

Metric Conversion Charts

Knitting Needles Conversion Chart

Canada/U.S.	0	1	2	3	4	5	6	7	8	9	10	10½	11	13	15
Metric (mm)	2	2¼	2¾	3¼	3½	3¾	4	4½	5	5½	6	6½	8	9	10

Crochet Hooks Conversion Chart

Canada/U.S.	1/B	2/C	3/D	4/E	5/F	6/G	8/H	9/I	10/J	10½/K	N
Metric (mm)	2.25	2.75	3.25	3.5	3.75	4.25	5	5.5	6	6.5	9.0

Metric Conversions

yards	x	.9144	=	metres (m)
yards	x	91.44	=	centimetres (cm)
inches	x	2.54	=	centimetres (cm)
inches	x	25.40	=	millimetres (mm)
inches	x	.0254	=	metres (m)
centimetres	x	.3937	=	inches
metres	x	1.0936	=	yards

Standard Abbreviations

[ ] work instructions within brackets as many times as directed
( ) work instructions within parentheses in the place directed
** repeat instructions following the asterisks as directed
* repeat instructions following the single asterisk as directed
" inch(es)

approx approximately
beg begin/beginning
CC contrasting color
ch chain stitch
cm centimeter(s)
cn cable needle
dec decrease/decreases/decreasing
dpn(s) double-pointed needle(s)
g gram
inc increase/increases/increasing

k knit
k2tog knit 2 stitches together
LH left hand
lp(s) loop(s)
m meter(s)
M1 make one stitch
MC main color
mm millimeter(s)
oz ounce(s)
p purl
pat(s) pattern(s)
p2tog purl 2 stitches together
psso pass slipped stitch over
p2sso pass 2 slipped stitches over
rem remain/remaining
rep repeat(s)
rev St st reverse stockinette stitch
RH right hand
rnd(s) rounds
RS right side

skp slip, knit, pass stitch over—one stitch decreased
sk2p slip 1, knit 2 together, pass slip stitch over the knit 2 together—2 stitches have been decreased
sl slip
sl 1k slip 1 knitwise
sl 1p slip 1 purlwise
sl st slip stitch(es)
ssk slip, slip, knit these 2 stitches together—a decrease
st(s) stitch(es)
St st stockinette stitch/stocking stitch
tbl through back loop(s)
tog together
WS wrong side
wyib with yarn in back
wyif with yarn in front
yd(s) yard(s)
yfwd yarn forward
yo yarn over

Modular Knitting Made Easy is published by DRG, 306 East Parr Road, Berne, IN 46711, telephone (260) 589-4000. Printed in USA. Copyright © 2009 DRG. All rights reserved. This publication may not be reproduced in part or in whole without written permission from the publisher.

RETAIL STORES: If you would like to carry this pattern book or any other DRG publications, call the Wholesale Department at Annie's Attic to set up a direct account: (903) 636-4303. Also, request a complete listing of publications available from DRG.

Every effort has been made to ensure that the instructions in this pattern book are complete and accurate. We cannot, however, take responsibility for human error, typographical mistakes or variations in individual work.

STAFF
Editor: Jeanne Stauffer
Assistant Editor: Erika Mann
Technical Editor: Kathy Wesley
Technical Artist: Pam Gregory
Copy Supervisor: Michelle Beck
Copy Editosr: Amanda Ladig
Graphic Arts Supervisor: Ronda Bechinski
Graphic Artists: Erin Augsburger, Debby Keel
Art Director: Brad Snow
Assistant Art Director: Nick Pierce
Photography Supervisor: Tammy Christian
Photography: Matt Owen
Photo Stylist: Tammy Steiner

ISBN: 978-1-59217-275-7
1 2 3 4 5 6 7 8 9

Inches into Millimeters & Centimeters

All measurements are rounded off slightly.

inches	mm	cm	inches	cm	inches	cm	inches	cm	inches	cm
⅛	3	0.3	3	7.5	13	33.0	26	66.0	39	99.0
¼	6	0.6	3½	9.0	14	35.5	27	68.5	40	101.5
⅜	10	1.0	4	10.0	15	38.0	28	71.0	41	104.0
½	13	1.3	4½	11.5	16	40.5	29	73.5	42	106.5
⅝	15	1.5	5	12.5	17	43.0	30	76.0	43	109.0
¾	20	2.0	5½	14	18	46.0	31	79.0	44	112.0
⅞	22	2.2	6	15.0	19	48.5	32	81.5	45	114.5
1	25	2.5	7	18.0	20	51.0	33	84.0	46	117.0
1¼	32	3.8	8	20.5	21	53.5	34	86.5	47	119.5
1½	38	3.8	9	23.0	22	56.0	35	89.0	48	122.0
1¾	45	4.5	10	25.5	23	58.5	36	91.5	49	124.5
2	50	5.0	11	28.0	24	61.0	37	94.0	50	127.0
2½	65	6.5	12	30.5	25	63.5	38	96.5		

Photo Index

16

28

12

39

24

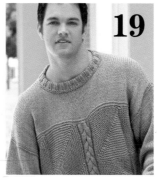

31

6

10

19

44

42

34